I0626745

BE, LIVE, DO
AMAZING!
The Kids' Guide to Life

To:

Note:

From:

*Not even
wise men can
be perfect.*
Toegye

*I am better off
than he is—for he knows
nothing, and thinks that he
knows. I neither know nor
think that I know.*
Socrates/Plato

*You simply
must have an
open mind.*
Zhu

Contents

As in
a game of cards,
so the game of life,
we must play what
is dealt to us.
Billings

Light is the
task when many
share the toil.
Homer

__Tribute__

I dedicate this to all kids.

To all innocents, for better or for

worse, who had zero control over how,

where, when, or why they were brought in

to this world; it is absolutely, not your fault.

You are a gift who deserves **AMAZING!**

Trustworthy adults can help you.

Play what you're dealt.

I further celebrate all of

the heroes who care about kids.

I applaud family, neighbors, teachers,

counselors, coaches, and others helping

children survive and thrive on this earth.

Be the right person, in the right place,

at the right time, living your life

doing the right thing.

Two things
stand like stone,
kindness in other's
trouble, courage
in your own.
Gordon

Love gives
life within.
Hawaiian
Adage

<u>Thanks</u>

Huge thanks go out to
our family, friends, co-workers,
and heroes helping with **AMAZING!**
Lo, one neighbor/teacher saved my life.
Instead of me studying for my 9th grade
geometry tests doing boilermakers
with dead people, she tutored
me from a D- to an A+.

Maui was my home.
Not my birthplace, my place
of residence... it was my home. I
fell madly in love and made my babies.
Maui is very beautiful, yet what I loved
most, were the people. They see
you for what you are, inside.
Mahalo Nui Loa Maui.

***Some things
are in our control
and others not.***
Epictetus

***When life
gives you lemons,
make lemonade.***
Hubbard

Preface

I used to really love my life.
I got paid to do exciting things and
help people! I was a firefighter on Maui
with two great kids, 13 and 10. Then they
saw their dear mother suffer a heart attack
and die six days later. Their aunty tried
to help, but then she had a stroke.
Then my dad got cancer.

So here I am writing to you.
We chose to make the best of it all,
and make lotsa lemonade. We followed
all the signs leading us to grandpa. I would
be there for him during his final years, help
my kids thrive, and write. Good choices
do make life easier—but not easy!
I hope it's truly **AMAZING!**

*Don't
make it too long!
They won't read it.*
Neighbor/Teacher
Molly

*From a
little spark may
burst a flame.*
Dante

Intro

I wrote this to help others.
I want to save young people from
tragic death, injury, and illness. I hope
to stop their imprisonment, homelessness,
addiction, and misery. I aspire to help kids
help themselves to live their best lives
possible, for their own good, and
for the good of the world.

The cures for afflictions,
peace, freedoms, and rule of law
will take far longer without all our gifts
and focus. I dream this will help most or
all, survive life's hazards and dead ends,
then thrive their healthiest, happiest,
best lives possible. I want you to
BE, LIVE, DO AMAZING!

Be AMAZING!

Who you are is your first step.

Nothing means anything if you're dark

and decaying at core level. Nice, integrous

people naturally attract, inspire, and bring out

the best in others. People in our lives can be

positive, neutral, or negative. Often, they

really love to help amazing people.

Be helped and **Be AMAZING!**

Be Nice!

Be Integrous!

*Respect for
ourselves guides
our morals; respect
for others guides
our manners.*
Sterne

*He that
plants thorns
must never expect
to gather roses.*
Sharma

*Be sure
to put your feet
in the right place,
and stand firm.*
Lincoln

Be Nice!

Being nice is the right way

and wisest way to be. Unjustly

hurting others is mean and cruel, and

reaps indifference or retribution as sown.

We create our own fortune or misfortune

via basic interactions. Brighten lives,

warm hearts, and make friends

and allies, and BE Nice!

Be Polite & Respectful
Be courteous, considerate, and classy.
Make your world a better place
one person at a time.

Be Kind & Caring
Be good-natured, warm-hearted, and loving.
Share your light and warmth to fully
realize the best in others.

Be Courageous & Strong
Be brave, thick-skinned, and rock-steady.
Find your way without being their
doormat or punching bag.

*Character is
much easier kept
than recovered.*

Paine

*To thine own
self be true, and it must
follow, as the night the day,
thou canst not then be
false to any man.*

Shakespeare

*Only the
just man enjoys
peace of mind.*

Epicurus

B<small>E</small> Integrous!

Being integrous is the right way
and wisest way to be. Lying, cheating,
and stealing are virtually always wrong, and
harm you, your people, success, and freedom.
Building trust and being just pay great benefits
personally, professionally, and legally. Bask
in righteousness for peace, prosperity,
and ease, and B<small>E</small> Integrous!

Be Honest & Trustworthy
Be respectable, honorable, and true-blue.
Make your word solid gold and your
reputation sterling silver.

Be Loyal & Dependable
Be genuine, faithful, reliable, and super solid.
Be a rock who says what they do and
does what they say.

Be Right-Minded & Fair
Be righteous, upstanding, and mutualistic.
Do and stand up for the right thing
for your win-win world.

14

Live AMAZING!

How you're living is your next step.
Nothing means anything if you're dying
disastrously at meso level. Wise, healthy,
happy people look after matters they control
or influence, and release all the rest. Often,
worry fades, hope grows, and a life of joy,
empowerment, and freedom begins.
Live free and Live AMAZING!

Live Wise!

Live Healthy!

Live Happy!

*Better to
be wise by the
misfortunes of
others than by
your own.*
Aesop

*If you hang
around crows in
the cornfield, you're
bound to get shot.*
Grandpa/Dad
McKie

*Look twice
before you leap.*
Bronte

17

L<small>IVE</small> Wise!

Living wise is the right way
and wisest way to live. Wasting,
wrecking, or ending your life foolishly
hurts you, your family, friends, and allies.
Wise living could limit preventable death,
destruction, and suffering. Control or
influence hazards, circles, and
choices, and L<small>IVE</small> Wise!

Avoid Traps & Addictions
Beware of violence, drugs, sex, and vice.
Learn from others (threats & errors)
to sidestep life's hazards.

See Assets & Liabilities
Escape/retreat from dangerous/toxic circles.
True friends/allies make you smarter,
healthier, happier… better.

Weigh Risks & Gains
Analyze danger/cost versus reward/benefit.
Risk wisely (big picture & long term)
to make good choices.

*Those who
don't find time for
exercise, must find
time for illness.*
Stanley

*An ounce of
prevention is worth
a pound of cure.*
Franklin

*Take rest;
a field that has
rested returns
a bounty.*
Ovid

L<small>IVE</small> **Healthy!**

Living healthy is the right way
and wisest way to live. Health and
wellness will never be taken for granted,
once they are gone. The gift of sound body,
mind, and soul is a treasure to truly cherish
and protect. Parlay PT, TLC, and R & R
into life vigor, vitality, quantity, and
quality, and L<small>IVE</small> **Healthy!**

Prioritize Exercise & Fitness
Enjoy physical, mental, and emotional benefits.
Physically train, breathe, and flow in the
peace and healing of nature.

Practice Self Care & Maintenance
Ease/lose inflammation and seek/find wellness.
Treat your body, mind, and soul with
tender loving care.

Utilize Rest & Recuperation
Sleep well, relax, and reconnect to reinvigorate.
Ignoring basic human needs yields the
law of diminishing returns.

The more man
meditates on good
thoughts, the better
will be his world.
Confucius

To err is human,
to forgive, divine.
Pope

Know thyself.
Nothing in excess.
Seven Sages

Live Happy!

Living happy is the right way

and wisest way to live. Grudges

and grievances fester and ooze, while

venom and vitriol poison and putrefy. For

however long it lasts, for everyone with no

chance, dare to lead your happiest life.

Choose, seek, and grow yourself

happy, and Live Happy!

Leverage Choice & Lifestyle
Choose joy, gratitude, love, and connection.
Happy begins with your inner world
and your greatest power.

Minimize Disruptions & Distractions
Seek peace, forgiveness, simplicity, and frugality.
Eliminate/mitigate the unhappy of your
inner and outer worlds.

Embrace Exploration & Discovery
Grow interests, abilities, personality, and values.
For lasting happy, learn/listen to your
body, mind, and soul.

22

<u>Do AMAZING!</u>

What you're doing is your last step.
Nothing means anything if you're barely
surviving at outer level. Successful, helpful
people try and fail upwards till thriving and up.
Their fear of never trying eclipses their fear of
ever failing. Often, pivotal success arises
from doing good and helping others.
Do help and **Do AMAZING!**

Do Succeed!

Do Help!

*Forewarned,
forearmed; to be
prepared is half
the victory.*

Cervantes

*Perseverance,
secret of all triumphs.*

Hugo

*Experience
shows that success
is due less to ability
than to zeal.*

Buxton

25

D<small>o</small> Succeed!

Succeeding is the right thing
and wisest thing to do. You cannot
help to your fullest potential if you never
realize your fullest potential. Improve and
move to your personal best to grow more
special, masterful, and free. Maximize
preparation, habits, and attitude to
truly soar, and **D<small>o</small> Succeed!**

Become Valuable & Powerful
Fortify via education, training, and adventure.
Knowledge + Skills + Experiences =
Preparation to Succeed.

Embody Hard & Smart Working
Commit and persevere while alert and flexible.
Persistence + Awareness + Agility =
Habits to Succeed.

Personify Positive & Professional
Show up, lift up, synergize, solve, and serve.
Aptitude + Attitude x Multiplier =
Attitude to Succeed.

What you
are stands over you
thundering, so I can't
hear what you say
to the contrary.
Emerson

Learn by
hearing is good.
Learn by seeing is
better. Learn by
doing is best.
Xunzi

Give a fish,
feed for a day.
Teach how to fish,
feed for life.
Ritchie

Do Help!

Helping is the right thing
and wisest thing to do. As the
end nears, questions bother people.
Who were you? How did you live? And,
whom did you help? Helping feels good,
and often gives and lives on. Show,
tell, and sell others how to help
themselves, and **Do Help!**

Be Admirable & Accessible
Be exemplary, egoless, and approachable.
Lead by example, stay grounded,
and show the way.

Be Influential & Transformative
Open eyes, save lives, and raise life quality.
Share knowledge, skills, wisdom,
and tell the way.

Be Supportive & Creative
Advocate, donate, improve, and originate.
Contribute time, energy, money,
and sell the way.

Knowing isn't
good enough; we
must apply. Willing
isn't good enough;
we must do.
Goethe

As you start
to walk on the way,
the way appears.
Rumi

Act
as if what you do
matters. It does.
James

AMAZING!

	BE			LIVE		DO	
	Nice!	Integrous!	Wise!	Healthy!	Happy!	Succeed!	Help!
	Be Polite & Respectful	Be Honest & Trustworthy	Avoid Traps & Addictions	Prioritize Exercise & Fitness	Leverage Choice & Lifestyle	Become Valuable & Powerful	Be Admirable & Accessible
	Be Kind & Caring	Be Loyal & Dependable	See Assets & Liabilities	Practice Self Care & Maintenance	Minimize Disruptions & Distractions	Embody Hard & Smart Working	Be Influential & Transformative
	Be Courageous & Strong	Be Right-Minded & Fair	Weigh Risks & Gains	Utilize Rest & Recuperation	Embrace Exploration & Discovery	Personify Positive & Professional	Be Supportive & Creative

Great journeys
take courage to start,
perseverance to continue,
keen awareness to adjust,
and agility to finish.

James McKie

Destiny is not
a matter of chance;
it is a matter of choice.
Not a thing to be waited
for, it is a thing to
be achieved.

Bryan

Insight

Your journey is unique.
Happiness and success for one
may be misery and failure for another.
Your interests, strengths, personality, and
values help ideate your anti-vision, vision,
mission, and purpose, and vice versa.
Learn from others and by doing
(trial & error), then adjust.

Dreams create destiny.
Set, plan, and achieve them by
identifying, prioritizing, and focusing
goals, parts, steps, tasks, and tweaks by
importance, urgency, sequence, or ease.
What doesn't work leads to what will.
Lists, calendars, boards… aid
with your **AMAZING!**

*Advance
confidently in the
direction of dreams,
and endeavor to live
the life which you
have imagined.*

Thoreau

*The only
failure man ought
to fear, is the failure to
cleave to the purpose
he sees to be best.*

Eliot

__Outro__

Your journey and destiny await.

The way forward and upward glows.

You're the single most powerful person

in your short life that goes way too fast.

Seize control, then direct discipline,

dedication, determination, and

diligence at dreams.

Dream, plan, and act!

Quell doubts/fears/obstacles

and seek careers/callings/destiny.

College, trade, jobs, business, books,

video, audio, mentor… keep learning.

Learn, think, dream, be, live, and

do super big with less regret.

Obsess for **AMAZING!**

**To be
good, and to
do good, is all
we must do.**

Adams

**A loving
heart maintains
a family; a hateful
heart destroys it.**

Shuruppak

Postface

Prevention trumps cure.

"Do no harm" is sage for any age.

Facts, integrity, values, risk reduction,

and trustworthy adults should guide you.

Never limit yourself. Try, fail, learn, then

triumph! Our late brother showed us

what not to do. Maybe John can

save a few more lives.

So I still love my life.

Generations sandwiching me

was hard, but you gotta believe your

best days lie ahead. Thanks to my son,

I ken a jet pilot. Thanks to my daughter,

I'll know a financial advisor. Thanks

to neighbor/teacher Barbara,

life's pretty **AMAZING!**

***Beauty will
save the world.***

Dostoyevsky

***Yes,
stand a bit out
of my sunshine.***

Diogenes

<u>Musing</u>

Who saved whom?

Our dog BB was **AMAZING!**

Black Beauty's joy, light, and love

eased our sadness, gloom, and loss.

What is a good life, probed Socrates.

To live simply in accordance with

nature, mused Antisthenes

the Cynic (Dog-Like).

They say you're not

truly a writer till you've killed

your favorite character. I believe

the opposite is true as well. My last

heuristic, final pages, my final book,

elevates my least favorite Lover

of Sophia, gifting him Telos.

Story is a tyrant.

Life can be hard sometimes.
We could all use a little help.
Comprehensive and concise,
life-saving and life-changing,

BE, LIVE, DO
AMAZING!

The Kids' Guide to Life

Bulk Discounts

Merchandise Soon

SupaBigs.com